D1239814

EVERYONE CAN BE A CHANGEMAKER:

THE ASHOKA EFFECT

Christine Welldon

Fitzhenry & Whiteside

Published in Canada by Fitzhenry & Whiteside,
195 Allstate Parkway, Markham, ON L3R 4T8

Published in the United States by Fitzhenry & Whiteside,
311 Washington Street, Brighton, Massachusetts 02135

www.fitzhenry.ca   godwit@fitzhenry.ca

10 9 8 7 6 5 4 3 2 1

Fitzhenry & Whiteside acknowledges with thanks the Canada Council
for the Arts, and the Ontario Arts Council for their support of our
publishing program.

We acknowledge the financial support of the Government of Canada
through the Canada Book Fund (CBF) for our publishing activities.

Library and Archives Canada Cataloguing in Publication
Everyone Can Be a Changemaker:
The Ashoka Effect / Christine Welldon.
ISBN 978-1-55455-357-0 (bound)
Data available on file

1. Social reformers--Biography--Juvenile literature. 2. Social
entrepreneurship--Juvenile literature. 3. Ashoka Changemakers--
Juvenile literature. I. Title.

HV27.W45 2016   j361.7'40922   C2016-901235-2

Publisher Cataloging-in-Publication Data (U.S.)
Names: Welldon, Christine, author.

Title: Everyone can be a changemaker :
Ashoka / Christine Welldon.

Description: Markham, Ontario Fitzhenry & Whiteside, 2018 | Includes
Index. | Summary: "Ashoka follows sixteen innovative kids
and adults and their goals for positive change. From harnessing clean energy
for developing countries to building playgrounds for children of all needs,
these inspiring individuals are changing the world one dream at a time.
Learn about how they've made global changes and how you can start your
own initiative" – Provided by publisher.

Identifiers: ISBN 978-1-55455-357-0 (paperback)
Subjects: LCSH: Social change – Juvenile literature. | Ashoka Innovators
for the Public (Organization) – Juvenile literature. | Social action – Juvenile
literature. | BISAC: JUVENILE NONFICTION / Social Topics / General.

Classification: LCC HM831.W452 |DDC 303.484 – dc23
Text and cover design by Tanya Montini
Front cover image courtesy of Ashoka Canada
Printed in Canada by Houghton Boston

"BE THE CHANGE YOU WISH TO SEE IN THE WORLD."

Mahatma Gandhi

TABLE OF CONTENTS

INTRODUCTION

Some people will be quick to tell you that there is no hope for change in the world, while others are certain that there is. Which side are you on?

If you believe there is hope to make the world a better place, you have vision. You can see the big picture. Perhaps you are thinking about a change you would like to see and are wondering how to make it happen. You also might see problems that could get in your way, but even though you don't see the solutions right away, you know there are people who can help.

There are thousands of changemakers in the world—social entrepreneurs who have found their way around problems and roadblocks in their quest for positive change. This book looks at only a few of these boys, girls, men, and women. From lighting jungle villages to building the perfect playground, each one has accomplished amazing work while striving to achieve their goals.

With the help of an organization called Ashoka, each changemaker discovered a network of other social entrepreneurs just like themselves. Each one benefitted from the encouragement, advice, and assistance of others within the network.

Ashoka is one of many helping agencies in the world that supports people who have a dream—to build on their ideas and accomplish even more; to make the world a better place, one step at a time.

Changemakers offer creative solutions to serious social problems around the world. Often known as "social entrepreneurs," these innovative people notice when things are "stuck" and find ways to get them "unstuck." They share their solutions with other communities and encourage others to take giant leaps to effect change.

The name Ashoka has history behind it. In 269 BC, King Ashoka the Great already ruled most of India, but that wasn't enough for him. This fierce and cruel king was intent on expanding his power and his land. He waged a bloody war on the peaceful people of Kalinga, located on the east coast of India. It was a war based on sheer greed for power. After the battle was won, Ashoka walked among the hundreds of thousands of people who lay dead or dying, but rather than feeling satisfied, he was bitterly ashamed of himself.

"What have I done?" he asked himself. "Is this a victory or a defeat? Is it valiant to kill innocent children and women? Did I do it to widen the empire and bring prosperity or to destroy the others' kingdom and splendour?"

The experience changed King Ashoka from a cruel ruler to a kind and loving one. He converted to Buddhism and asked that his people practise goodness, virtue, and charity. He constructed pillars that still exist today and are known as the Pillars of Ashoka. On them, he wrote his messages of peace and love for people of all religions.

Today, the practice of goodness, virtue, and charity is the aim of the helping agency known as Ashoka, named after that famous king of long ago. Ashoka is a worldwide network of mentors and fundraisers who assist changemakers to reach their goals. Before joining Ashoka, each changemaker had already discovered something that needed to be put right in their community or in the world around them. Through perseverance and problem solving, they have found ways to make change happen.

Ashoka, with its motto "Everyone a Changemaker," offers mentorship and financial help to changemakers around the world so that they can accomplish even more.

The Ashoka network exists in every corner of the world, and to date it has helped more than three thousand social entrepreneurs in seventy countries through its funding and mentoring programs. The people you will read about here are only a few of the thousands of changemakers who are creating change for the good of everyone.

CHAPTER 1

TOMAS LANG
Burnaby, British Columbia, Canada

Think Outside the Trash

"When I see someone throw something into a waste bin, I feel it's morally wrong," says high-school student Tomas Lang.

Tomas does not enjoy seeing plastic knives and forks thrown into the recycling bin every time there is a food event at his high school. He knows that polystyrene plastic does not get recycled. Furthermore, it takes centuries to break down plastic in landfill sites.

"It's not good enough to recycle," says Tomas. "We need to reduce before we can recycle."

THE CLOCK IS TICKING

Tomas found a solution to the "throw away" habits he observed among those around him. Though most school libraries contain books and computers, Tomas has created a different kind of library; one that contains plates, forks, tumblers, and knives. Thanks to Tomas, the Reusable Events Materials Library is a resource that has changed the way schools deal with waste. Sure, he knows that teachers do their part to teach about reducing, reusing, and recycling, but more action is needed, and time is running out. Landfill sites are growing and are spreading contaminants into the groundwater. Greenhouse gases are polluting the air.

"Teachers can't change things as fast as students can. They're tied down by rules and bureaucracy," says Tomas. "Students aren't as tied down by rules. They're free to imagine. This is change from the bottom up rather than the top down."

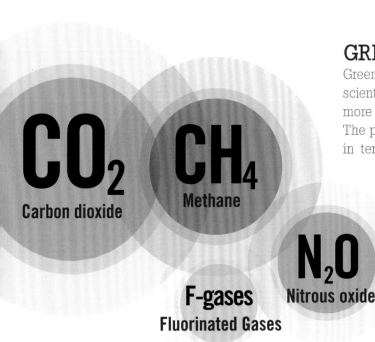

CO₂
Carbon dioxide

CH₄
Methane

N₂O
Nitrous oxide

F-gases
Fluorinated Gases

GREENHOUSE GASES (GHG)

Greenhouse gas happens naturally, but scientists agree that it is people who are putting more and more gases into the atmosphere. The planet is becoming warmer, and this rise in temperature could be very dangerous for our planet. You can do your part to lessen the effects of greenhouse gas. Walk or bike, take a bus or train instead of driving a car, recycle waste and use a composter, and turn off the lights when you are not using them.

A YOUNG NATURALIST

Tomas's passion for conservation began at a young age. He grew up in a family that was always concerned about the environment.

"When I was a child, we had a composter in the garden. I used to go to Young Naturalists Club meetings. My parents are veterinarians and we would go on outings to observe local wildlife in the lakes and woods," remembers Tomas. "That was the way my family lived. We were always closely connected to the environment."

These early interests have stayed with Tomas. Thanks to his initiative, Burnaby High School enjoyed its first Green Event, where students held a pancake breakfast in the gym. Tables were laden with not just pancakes, but stacks of china plates, bowls of metal knives and forks, and signs directing students on how to separate used utensils.

"It looked better. It looked cleaner. It was awesome because so much less garbage was created. Over the course of the school year, we got 2,500 uses of these plates, forks, and knives."

That effort meant that thousands of plastic items did not end up in a landfill site.

"Undertaking this initiative wasn't an easy ride," cautions Tomas. "Not everyone gave me 100 percent support at the beginning."

But with persistence and dedication to his cause, Tomas has won the support of the students and staff at his school and wants to build on his success and get the message out to other schools. His vision is to see more schools get on board and, whenever possible, to reuse before they recycle.

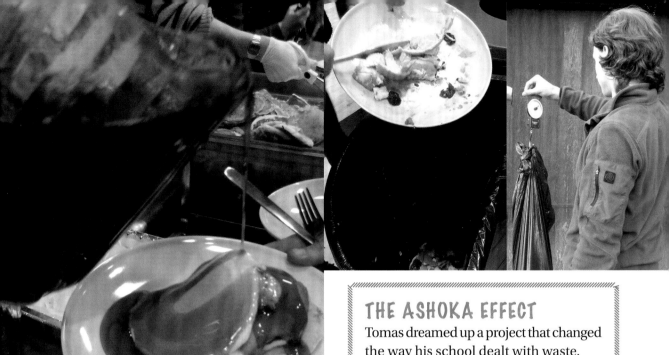

A LITTLE BIT OF THOUGHT

"I encourage my friends to think about what they're using; to bring reusable bottles rather than disposable water bottles to school," says Tomas. And as for the future, "I feel sustainability and environmental issues will be a part of any career I decide to pursue."

Would you like to start a green project at your school? Do you have some doubts that you can do it? Tomas has good advice for you. "If you think you have an idea for a project, try talking to your school's environment club, your teachers, principals, parents, and friends. Lots of people are out there to help you achieve your goals—you just need to reach out and ask for help."

"Working on a project is a rewarding experience," says Tomas. "You will learn skills like leadership, perseverance, and creative problem solving—skills which will stick with you for your whole life."

THE ASHOKA EFFECT

Tomas dreamed up a project that changed the way his school dealt with waste.

Ashoka helped him to bring his idea to other school communities through Youth Venture, an international community of young changemakers.

A branch of Ashoka called Youth Venture helps teams of young people, such as the one Tomas and his friends have formed, develop and launch their own creative ideas to help solve the problems around them.

Tomas speaks excitedly about the program that has helped him to change not only his own school community, but that of others as well. "Ashoka helped me with a grant and mentored me through their Youth Venture Program," he explains. He hopes that others, like him, will dream it, then do it!

The Youth Venture program has a mission to help people like Tomas to implement their solutions through collaboration, enrichment, and mentorship-to build a membership of young people who are being powerful now.

CHAPTER 2

EDEN FULL
Calgary, Alberta, Canada

Courage, Google, & Love

Whenever Eden Full took a day off from high school, it wasn't because she didn't feel like going. It was because she wanted to continue tinkering on a project in the basement: an amazing solar invention of her own making. Although she didn't yet know it, her rotating solar panel was an invention destined to bring alternative energy and clean water to communities on the other side of the world. She would call it the SunSaluter.

"Start small!" is Eden Full's advice to anyone interested in helping our planet. "Never be overwhelmed by the big problems of climate change. Tackle something small in your own life."

That is exactly what Eden did.

A BUDDING SCIENTIST

As a child, Eden loved to build things, and she had a hungry curiosity about the world around her. Eden's dad frequently brought home photographs and current events news clippings from his work at a Calgary newspaper. Eden was fascinated by images of Mars Exploration Rovers and other technology, as well as the stories and pictures about interesting people and the work they did. She absorbed everything, always questioning and curious. She was only three when she told her father she knew exactly what she wanted to do with her life—to be a scientist.

"You can make a difference," encouraged her father. "Give it your passion, and you can be anything you want to be."

At the age of nine, Eden assembled a model solar-powered car from a kit that her mother had given her, but its battery had limited energy. The car would go from one end of the room to the other, then stop. Eden explored ways she could get maximum energy out of its solar panel to make the car run for a longer time. She Googled "solar panels," and learned everything she could.

A trip to Home Depot with her dad to pick up components resulted in a prototype of a solar panel that rotated to track the path of the sun across the sky. By following the sun, the panel was able to absorb maximum solar energy without using a motor. She was ten when she entered the device into an international science fair. There, someone commented that her device could help people in faraway rural villages that had no electricity. Inspired, she turned her thoughts to finding practical uses for her invention—applications that would help make people's lives better. Where might her technology be needed most?

She continued refining the device as she completed high school. Her parents wanted her to go to university, and she knew further education would give her the grounding in mechanical engineering that she needed. It was time to find the right university.

One of Eden's mottoes is "Apply. Apply. Then apply again!" She already knew her place in the universe: she was destined for a career in science. She applied for scholarships to at least fifty universities, highlighting her current work on the SunSaluter. She was delighted to be offered a place at Princeton University.

> She showed the people how her invention worked and how they could build their own with materials at hand.

LIGHTING THE NIGHT

In 2010, a summer internship led Eden to visit Kenya. She brought her SunSaluter with her. She showed the people how her invention worked and how they could build their own with materials at hand. Two villages used and benefit from her project. They spread the word, and soon, one thousand people without electricity could power their lanterns when night fell.

Eden also noticed that the villagers had no access to clean, filtered water. By tweaking the SunSaluter's design, she added a water-filtering capability. Easy to use and cheap to make, the invention solved two problems in one.

As a social entrepreneur, Eden needed funding to work on refinements, so she sent out multiple applications looking for connections.

"Find them on LinkedIn, and get connections to people who have experience," she advises. "Cast a wide net. See how many fish you get."

Her diligence paid off. In 2011, Eden won the grand prize of Ashoka's Staples Youth Social Entrepreneur Award—a competition that invites youth from around the world to offer solutions to social issues. That same year, she won a Thiel Fellowship, which provided her with the means to bring her product to the marketplace...but there was a catch. To accept the funding, Eden would have to drop out of Princeton for two years. She knew her parents would be concerned, but she promised them she would return to Princeton after the two years were up.

In 2012, Eden was named one of the Top 30 under 30 in Forbes' Energy category. All of these grants allowed her to travel the world, collaborate with others, and connect with mentors. Today, there are a total of two hundred SunSaluters installed in the countries of Kenya, Uganda, and Tanzania, bringing clean water and solar energy to 15,000 villagers and counting.

KEEP BELIEVING

"If you care about something, if you want something badly enough, there are always ways to get it," advises Eden. "Worrying about any kind of constraints limits you. Always believe there is a solution. Find your place in the universe. Find your passion. Google for information. Have courage. Love! You're never too young to start."

Eden assures you it's not hard. Start small. Find something in your home or environment that needs to change. Google it. How does it work? What do you need? Like Eden, you too can effect change to make the world a better place.

THE ASHOKA EFFECT

"Ashoka gave me my very first grant," enthuses Eden, "when I had no credits, no experience, and I hadn't done anything. The project has grown. That initial bit of encouragement catalyzed my passion—gave me a platform to start expressing how I want to change the world."

With Ashoka's help, Eden is installing SunSaluters in nine more countries.

STEVE LEAFLOOR
Windsor, Ontario, Canada

A Beatbox, a Back-spin, and a Buddha

If you watch Steve Leafloor give a presentation on his program Blueprint for Life, you instantly want to move to the rhythm and the beat. The audience gets a taste of his cool dance moves, the air is electric, and everyone is hooked. You can hear the truth in his voice and see the passion in his eyes. His childhood recollections resonate.

Who hasn't been bullied? Who hasn't been afraid to step up and make a change?

A BULLY SURVIVAL COURSE

Back in the early '80s, Steve was the new kid in a tough school. He knew the bullies were waiting for him. Being a short, skinny kid who was unsure of himself made him a prime target for the swaggering big kids who

made his life a daily hell. One time, they upended him into the cafeteria garbage can just as easily as they might throw away cold French fries. They gave him wedgies that ripped his underwear and threw the ripped pieces down the hall after him. He began to believe he was worthless.

Raging inside, he channeled his anger toward others. So his younger sister was taller than he? Time to make her life miserable, to make her pay. He was too young to realize there was a pattern here, that bullying begets more of the same. Eventually, he discovered a way to bounce back.

The dance music of the day was funk. All the cool guys hung out at the roller-skating rink and showed off their technique—a slow,

strutting dance that drew the girls. They had swag and Steve wanted some of that.

He watched closely; how to spin on one foot, do a round backhouse spin into the splits and finish with a locker jump. He practised hard in private, then tried his moves out in public. Now all eyes were on him—not to bully him but to admire his roller-skating moves. His confidence was still shaky, but he began to feel better about himself.

In the early '80s, people started to notice inner-city kids performing a dance called B-boying or breaking. It was one element of hip hop—a cultural movement that also included rap and graffiti art. Hip hop music was about expressing anger and despair through the lyrics of rap and the rhythm of beatboxing. It had lots to say, and it used vibrant, rapid-fire rhythms to say it. A scene in a Hollywood movie, *Flash Dance*, had everyone talking. It featured an amazing dance move: the backspin.

"How does that work?" Steve wondered as he watched the scene for the first time. "I need that move. It's got swag written all over it."

He watched the movie ten times. He practised the backspin, then conquered it. Hip hop became his new passion. He had discovered a simple formula: doing the positive things he loved—roller skating, dancing to funk, B-boying—helped enhance his feeling of self-worth and brought him joy.

BUILD YOUR TOOLKIT

At twenty years of age, Steve took a summer job in the wilderness mentoring a group of "problem" teenagers. By fishing with them, walking the land, and camping, Steve helped them learn new skills. He watched their attitudes change as they turned their thoughts away from their disappointments and failures. This was to be a turning point for Steve. He had once been just as angry as they were, but he'd swept away his negative feelings through dance.

He wanted to share that positive feedback loop and make a difference in the lives of others. He would help troubled youths to develop toolkits of their own.

He called it his "mindset survival toolkit." The idea was to replace the negative feelings with something positive by finding a passion or learning a skill, and adding new positive "feel-good" tools.

He studied for his master's degree in social work, and he became a B-boy with his own crew of dancers—Dexter, Beat Street, Tricky T, Kid Quick, and Coach. Because of his shaved head, stocky build, and warm laugh, his crew called Steve "Buddha." His dance team would rub Steve's stomach for good luck before going on stage. They became so good that they were the opening act for the likes of James Brown and rapper Ice-T.

TAKE A HEALING JOURNEY

As a childcare worker, Steve visited the Arctic for the first time. He discovered that the suicide rate there is eleven times higher than it is in the rest of Canada[1]. Children struggled with gas sniffing, physical and sexual abuse, drugs, and alcoholism. Many felt alienated, without pride in their heritage—lost children living in broken communities. He recognized their need to heal.

Here were angry youths whose stories were all similar. Their outlook was often dark. Steve thought he would tempt them with the coolness of B-boy dancing, then start them on a positive mindset—and start them early.

"At some point, you've got to grow past the anger. Ego or swag was important but when you're on a healing journey, you can't get stuck there in that place," says Steve. "So what's the next level? That's to give some meaning back and share—use your own personal story, inspire others."

To deliver his program, Steve embraced the ways of the Inuit culture, adapting their storytelling, throat singing, and traditional dancing and drumming to the hip hop routine.

It was hip hop, Inuit style.

The Inuit kids caught on in no time. Throat singing became throat boxing—a replacement for beatboxing. It was a non-aggressive way of saying, "You can sing that? Now it's my turn. Listen to how I can sing it." They came for the hip hop and stayed for the healing. Now they had a venue to talk openly about complex issues in their lives.

While graffiti is part of hip hop culture, the teens decided to put their own twist on it. "Graffiti?" they said. "Well, our buildings are covered in white frost. We don't have to vandalize buildings to make our messages. And we don't have to be negative. We'll create positive, affirmative messages in the frost."

When the Elders came out of their homes that morning, they saw buildings covered with frost graffiti that expressed good wishes, kind intentions, and had respectful and caring messages and pictures. The Elders had never before seen their kids so happy.

Steve was especially interested in the shy, withdrawn kids. They needed to first find some confidence in themselves.

"People are so hurt, they don't have the confidence for the first step. I suffered in

You might think the human voice can sing only one note at a time, but in throat singing, a singer sings two or more notes at the same time.

silence about being bullied. I couldn't tell my dad about it until I was in my twenties."

Steve helped these kids find their passion: go for walks on their land, hunt, fish, play sports—things to add to their toolkits to help them gain the confidence to share their troubles.

PREPARE YOUR BLUEPRINT

Has there been an Aha! moment in your life? An idea for your life path? What's in your toolkit? Positive skills that give you joy? If yes, keep it up! You're creating a Blueprint for Life. If your answer is no, here's Steve's advice for you:

"Find your passion and try to grow that a bit until your confidence grows and you can reach outside for help. Dance, play hockey—surround yourself with these activities as much as possible. Make a plan—a toolkit—to help you heal. Don't heal for anyone else. Heal for yourself. You deserve to be a happy human being."

THE ASHOKA EFFECT

"I'm excited that there are people who can help mentor me with ideas," says Steve. "At first it was, 'I don't have anybody to help me with my plan.' I was trying to figure it out by myself. It's great to have people in similar situations to share and learn from."

With the help of Ashoka and Boeringer Ingleheim, a health-care provider, Steve has reached four thousand people in seventy-five communities in the Arctic with his Blueprint for Life program. He has taken his program into Calgary prisons, and has worked with First Nations women who were mistreated in residential schools. Now, he would like to share his Blueprint with governments in other countries. There is no doubt that Steve can make it happen.

CLAUDIA LI
Vancouver, British Columbia, Canada

The Truth About Sharks

True or False?

"There is an abundance of sharks in the oceans, and they are a danger to humans."

If your answer was "True," you are one of the many thousands who believe all sharks are dangerous. If you chose "False," then good for you. You are already developing an awareness and empathy toward a misunderstood and threatened creature. The Shark Truth is that your chances of being killed by a shark are one in twelve million, yet over seventy-three million sharks are killed per year by humans[1].

Claudia Li is determined to help young Canadians develop empathy and awareness, not only for the environment, but for other cultures. Her program Shark Truth is helping to bring about social change.

CHICKEN FEET CHALLENGES

Claudia grew up in Canada and belongs to a large extended family whose members all immigrated to Canada from Hong Kong. Growing up with two cultures and learning to speak two languages created challenges for Claudia, as it might for any new Canadian. One painful memory stays with her even today.

One day, she happily shared with her friends that her favourite meat was chicken feet.

"Weird!" the children sneered and laughed. "Chicken feet! Ewwww!"

After school that day, Claudia's grandmother listened with sympathy to her story. "The children did not realize that it is our custom not to waste any part of the animals we eat," she gently explained to Claudia.

Claudia's grandmother would have won praise from conservationists today for the wisdom that she'd demonstrated. In 2012 alone, 600 million tons of food reached landfill sites and incinerators, and each year the numbers grow[2]. Such wasteful habits cause methane—a greenhouse gas even more destructive to our planet than carbon dioxide. Claudia had learned a lesson that day: perceived racial and cultural differences can act as barriers to communicating and sharing traditional wisdom among all people. She took this lesson with her through school, noticing over and over how visible minorities were treated differently, as though they did not belong. How could she improve cross-cultural understanding? How could she reconnect youth to their traditions and raise awareness for conservation issues?

While attending university, Claudia saw a film about shark finning: the practice of cutting off the fins of sharks for use in specially prepared soups at wedding banquets in Asia. Sharks are then tossed back into the ocean. She learned that sharks will become extinct if this practice continues. Fins are the sharks' steering mechanisms and without them, sharks cannot swim, dive, or hunt.

Without them, sharks die.

Claudia remembered her grandmother's words. Could she use her grandmother's wisdom to help save the sharks? Could she challenge young Canadians of every ethnic group to help right the wrongs they saw around them? Could she bridge the gap in understanding minority cultures and, at the same time, help the environment?

SHARKS ARE OUR FRIENDS, NOT FOOD AND THAT IS WHY WE HAVE PLEDGED NOT TO SERVE SHARK FIN SOUP AT OUR WEDDING.

HAPPY HEARTS LOVE SHARKS

Claudia's company Shark Truth does all this. Its members talk to youths and help make them aware of good conservation practices within their own culture. They have conversations with the youths about traditional values and how to respect these without harming the environment.

Through her program, Happy Hearts Love Sharks, she encourages young couples who are planning their weddings to also plan their menu in a way that does not harm or threaten our planet or the animals who live on it. Claudia encourages these young Asian-Canadian couples to replace shark fin soup with shark information. Instead of the traditional soup, the wedding couples place brochures on the table—literature that speaks of shark conservation. Then the couples talk to their guests about why they chose not to serve shark fin soup. As a result, guests begin to understand the dangers to sharks. They discuss the information amongst themselves and make their informed decisions. Many pledge to help stop the practice of shark finning.

Claudia urges all young Canadians to be aware of wrongs that they can put right in some small way.

"Life is about listening, not only with our ears, but also with our hearts," advises Claudia.

"You will fall and it will hurt—just know that it's normal. Do the work to find the love and support in your life and pick yourself back up. Keep moving forward."

As Claudia has demonstrated, it only takes one small step to help our planet. Look around you. What step will you take?

THE ASHOKA EFFECT

"Ashoka has surrounded me with thinkers, leaders, and entrepreneurs from all around the world to help me see my vision through," says Claudia. With Ashoka's help, she is encouraging many cultural groups to connect with others, achieve cultural pride, and respect the environment. Since she launched Shark Truth, at least eighty thousand bowls of shark fin soup have been stopped. Eight thousand people are now on board with Claudia's program. And the result? Shark Truth has saved at least eight thousand sharks!

Claudia continues to get her message out there, and with airtime on Canadian radio programs, she's educating tens of thousands of Canadians. Now that's success!

TAYLOR GUNN
Toronto, Ontario, Canada

Can You Spare a Vote?

It is Election Day!

There is excitement in the air. The voters are ready. They know each candidate's campaign promises. They're good citizens who take their responsibilities seriously. They've studied the issues and have discussed their opinions with family and friends. Now it's time to head to the polls.

Each voter enters the voting booth, marks a ballot with an X next to the candidate of their choice, and places it in the ballot box. All leave the polling station feeling proud to have taken part in the democratic process. After all, democracy is a precious resource—it represents freedom.

But wait! These voters are too young to vote! They're just kids. Their votes don't even count. So what is this all about?

It is all part of Student Vote, an idea created by Taylor Gunn to get kids involved in democracy and to ensure they understand the importance of the precious right to vote.

WHO CARES?

Voting is a freedom we should not take for granted. There are countries in the world whose citizens cannot vote. They live in a society where they have no voice in the running of their government. They are punished if they try to speak out against those who control them.

The big picture is grim. Many people in the world today do not have civic and political freedom. They are not allowed to vote for the leaders they would like to govern them.

In Canada and the United States, there is democracy, but the danger to democracy lies with citizens who don't bother to vote: citizens who are indifferent. As a result, there is a low voter turnout each Election Day. In Canada, voter turnout has been dropping since the year 2000. Today, only sixty-one percent of Canadians vote in federal elections[1]. The percentage is even lower in the United States[2]. The attitude is, "What difference can my vote make?"

It is a fact that the more educated people are, the more likely it is that they will vote. It seems that people with a higher level of education have been taught the importance of exercising this precious right.

YOUR VOTE COUNTS!

Taylor is doing some important teaching of his own. His campaign is to teach young people that the right to vote is a privilege. He knows that learning about the process at a young age provides the groundwork to establish good citizenship skills later.

Whenever Canadians prepare to vote in federal, provincial, or municipal elections, it is an exciting event for students to hold a "mock" Election Day at the same time. Taylor's program ensures that students can experience how it feels to be a responsible citizen and vote.

Schools that register for Taylor's Student Vote program receive a campaign package full of tools. There are campaign posters, electoral maps, voting screens, ballot boxes, and opportunities to hold debates and follow media reports. For weeks before Election Day, students discuss and debate the issues. When voting day comes at last, it is a time of excitement and anticipation. At the end of the day, student returning officers count the votes and announce the winners. The

There are countries in the world whose citizens cannot vote. They live in a society where they have no voice in the running of their government. They are punished if they try to speak out against those who control them.

school's election results are published in local newspapers and the media. Even though it is not the "real thing", participating in the Student Vote program is a valuable lesson in citizenship.

"I think that young people are reacting well to the program. They like it a lot—the dialogue with their peers and their parents," says Taylor. "Kids are saying, 'That was so much fun! When are we doing that again?'"

By helping young people realize the meaning of democracy, Taylor is making sure that when young citizens become old enough to vote, they will go to the polls on Election Day. They will take an interest in campaign promises and compare the pros and cons of each candidate before they make their

decision. He hopes that the kids involved in his program now will become responsible citizens later who know the value of making their voice heard.

The program has already created a ripple effect with the families of students. "The students are gaining confidence as they learn about political issues," Taylor observes. "They are talking to their parents and sharing opinions."

When a teacher commented that because of Student Vote, one of her older graduate students went to the polls and voted for the very first time, Taylor knew he was on the right track. He felt rewarded in his work to promote good citizenship.

"I'm doing something for people! I've

always been that way since I was young—doing something for other people in a variety of different ways. I always wanted to help. That was pretty clear. I felt whatever I did should be for the common good, not just for myself."

EYES ON THE GOAL

Taylor knows that when you have an idea to make a change, it sometimes takes a while to figure out how to make that idea work. He has good advice for children who are not sure about how to become changemakers. He understands that it is best to keep your eye on the goal. "I don't think there is a method or structure that you have to look for—just be yourself and approach things the way you want," says Taylor. "The goal comes first."

Taylor is doing exactly that. With initiatives like Student Vote, the future of Canadian democracy is in good hands.

THE ASHOKA EFFECT

"With Ashoka's help, I've been able to meet a network of Canadians that I'm very impressed by; a very interesting group of people tackling serious challenges that other people don't often think about," says Taylor. "It's very motivating, just to feel I've been allowed to be in their company. It's very rewarding and meaningful."

Student Vote has registered 4,300 schools in its program. Overall, more than 2 million students from across Canada have participated in these parallel elections. Taylor's next goal is to train teachers to deliver the program and encourage democratic participation within their school communities.

His campaign is to teach young people that the right to vote is a privilege. He knows that learning about the process at a young age provides the groundwork to establish good citizenship skills later.

Photo credit Timea Hajdrak

MANON BARBEAU
Montreal, Quebec, Canada

A Bridge to Understanding

Manon Barbeau would be the first to tell you that pictures speak louder than words. It is through the magic of filmmaking that she encourages young First Nations people to find their place in the world. She helps them restore a feeling of pride in their cultural identity. Through her work, the tribal memory of an almost forgotten yet precious heritage is being renewed.

Long ago, in the land now called Canada, First Nations people lived in harmony with the land. Children learned from their Elders about the importance of the wisdom, honesty, bravery, and love necessary to create peace and harmony in their lives. The people gave respect and thanks for the environment, animals, plants, sun and moon, and seasons.

CANADA'S SHAME

When European settlers arrived in Canada, everything changed for First Nations people. A "civilization" program destroyed their culture, brought death and disease, and forced them to change their beliefs and traditional ways. The children were removed from their homes to live at Indian Residential Schools. There, teachers cruelly punished children for speaking their own language, and forced children to abandon their cultural beliefs and traditions. For the next 150 years, First Nations children were physically and sexually abused and punished. Many died of disease and neglect. All lost connections to their language and traditions.

Manon began to use the power of filmmaking to bring attention to the suffering of street kids, homeless people, and other groups who are ignored by the more fortunate.

Since 1996, when the last residential school closed, there has been a time of building bridges of understanding—not only between Canadians and First Nations people, but also between First Nations children and their Elders. It is a sad fact that those traditions once taught by Elders to children have become lost. The language, beliefs, and proud heritage have all been severely damaged.

Manon Barbeau wants to help change this.

Manon felt very sad whenever she read or heard about racism. She grew up in Quebec, a province that is home to many First Nations tribes, and yet not many people could name even one such community. She was shocked to read about the high levels of suicide, drug abuse, violence, and school drop-outs among First Nations people, not only in Quebec but throughout Canada. When she was grown up, Manon began to use the power of filmmaking to bring attention to the suffering of street kids, homeless people, and other groups who are ignored by the more fortunate.

TELL YOUR STORY, LIVE YOUR DREAM

When her career in filmmaking brought her to an Atikamekw community in northern Quebec, Manon observed that the people there were enduring the hardships and despair typical of so many of Canada's First Nations people.

The Atikamekw were once a proud people known for crafting birch-bark canoes and baskets with beautiful designs. But when Manon visited this community, she saw that their land had been taken by logging companies, and their culture was almost extinct. Manon was determined to help them redefine themselves and give them hope. She decided to dedicate her life to this isolated tribe.

Manon was especially drawn to helping the Atikamekw youth. She knew she had to find a way to reach out to them, so she began to focus on these marginalized young people.

Storytelling was the way in.

Manon began to encourage young people to tell their stories through the medium of film. Her first documentary film about them was titled, *The End of Contempt*. It told the story of a young Atikamekw woman whose name was Wapikoni, who had overcome her losses and had achieved success in her life. By presenting this young woman's story on film, Manon hoped to empower the tribe and other First Nations communities, to help them overcome their feelings of humiliation and defeat, and to help them rediscover pride in their culture. Sadly, Wapikoni later died in a car accident, so Manon named her production company Wapikoni Mobile to honour her lost friend.

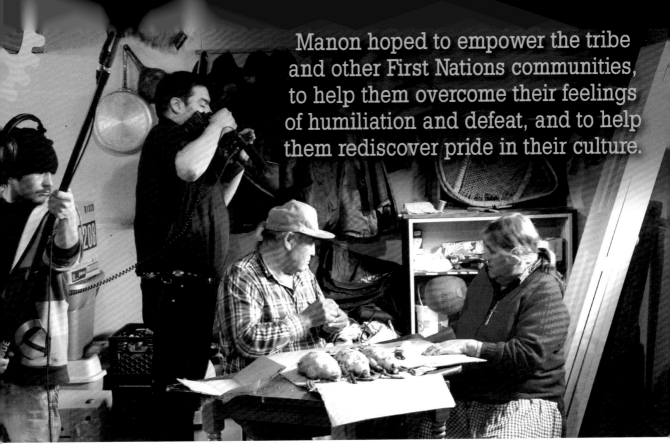

Manon hoped to empower the tribe and other First Nations communities, to help them overcome their feelings of humiliation and defeat, and to help them rediscover pride in their culture.

Manon began to widen her outreach. With her mobile film studio and a team of filmmakers and helpers, Manon now visits many different First Nations communities and teaches young people the art of scripting, acting, and producing their stories. While these stories often focus on painful issues, telling them serves to inspire confidence and strength in a people who seemed to have lost their way. The results are poignant films made by and for the people that not only help the generations connect, but that also help restore pride in Atikamekw heritage, and raise self-confidence and hope.

Manon has good advice for youths who feel isolated and have lost their feeling of belonging. "Every difficulty will come to an end if you stick to what you want. Difficulties nourish you and urge you on more strongly. It is important to keep your dreams. Nothing is impossible."

Manon's work is helping First Nations youths realize their dreams, accentuate the positive, and begin to heal. Many of the children's films have won national and international awards. With Manon's help, First Nations youths are finding their place in the world.

THE ASHOKA EFFECT

"Ashoka understands my goals," says Manon. "I felt less alone with this understanding. That is the main thing. And when you don't feel alone, that gives you the strength to push yourself forward."

With Ashoka's help, Manon is extending her outreach to other Canadian First Nations communities in Alberta and Manitoba, as well as to the aboriginal communities of Brazil, Bolivia, Peru, and French Polynesia.

CHAPTER 7

JEAN-FRANÇOIS ARCHAMBAULT
Montreal, Quebec, Canada

A Recipe for Living

When Jean-François Archambault began a career as a highly paid executive in the hotel industry, he was shocked at the amount of food he saw wasted every day.

"I couldn't believe so much food was being thrown away. That did not make any sense," says Jean-François.

Vegetables and meat that were not used that day went into the trash. Chefs' mistakes? Trash. Unused pasta sauces, the trim from cuts of meat, raw stems and leafs of fresh produce—so much food hit the dumpsters behind hotels and restaurants. So many things that were once potential meals were now consigned for the landfill site. And that meant more methane and more global warming.

Jean-François often noticed homeless people at the dumpsters behind hotels and restaurants picking through the discarded food. Chefs might call this food garbage, but for the homeless, it was a decent meal. *If only the food could go directly from the kitchen to the needy and not hit the dumpster at all*, Jean-François thought. He immediately began to envision a way to make this happen, but acting on it would mean leaving his high-paying job and changing his career path.

For many, this might seem too big a challenge, but for Jean-François, it was his destiny, pure and simple.

GROWING UP LUCKY

Jean-François considers himself lucky to have enjoyed a privileged childhood. His parents

taught him a recipe for life: community service is important—always look for ways to help those in need. They encouraged him to serve his community by helping in food drives, especially at Christmas time when the needy had trouble scraping together a holiday dinner.

The satisfaction Jean-François felt by helping others remained with him into adulthood, and now urged him toward a life-changing decision.

HELPING IS NOT A SPECTATOR SPORT

No longer would he stand by and watch so much good food being thrown away. Instead, he was determined to take action—to find a way to get that food to those in need as quickly as possible. Talking to chefs seemed a good place to start. He would find like-minded people who could help him achieve his vision.

But it was not to be an easy road. Those he spoke to expressed their worries.

"What if the food we donate is not fresh enough?" one chef asked. "We could be held liable if the quality is not good."

Others expressed the same concerns. "The food might become spoiled on its way from our kitchen to the people in need. We would be blamed for that," they said.

Jean-François assured them that the Good Samaritan Law would offer protection. As long as any food donations were made in good faith and in the spirit of helping those less fortunate, mistakes would be forgiven.

Once their fears were put to rest, many chefs stepped up to help and the *Tablée des Chefs* (Band of Chefs) was born. Jean-François quit his executive job, gave up his high salary, and jumped in to become an employee of his new organization.

The Band of Chefs saw their first success when they fed two thousand homeless people at one event. Partnering with the Bell Centre in Montreal, the chefs now had a venue for the needy to enjoy meals created with fresh ingredients directly from the kitchens—food that would otherwise have been thrown out.

With this success under their belt, the Band of Chefs continued to bring healthy, nutritious meals to the needy. During that year, they delivered sixty thousand meals to the underprivileged.

But the tireless chefs didn't stop there. It was time to ramp it up.

Over three million Canadians do not have enough money to properly feed their families. Many live with anxiety each day that there will not be enough food to stave off their hunger. This situation is known as "food insecurity."

EAT WELL, BE WELL

Jean-François knew that cooking classes were no longer offered in schools. As a result, children were not given the opportunity to learn about good nutrition. A diet of fast food with its high amounts of fat and salt was causing obesity among youth.

"We began bringing cooking classes into high schools," says Jean-François. "Once each week for six weeks, we go in and teach these children how to cook. They learn about good nutrition and how to prepare a basic meal with fresh ingredients. These are skills they will take with them into adulthood when they have a family of their own."

He remembers one thirteen-year-old boy eager to sign up for the Tuesday class.

"Why are you interested in signing up?" he asked the boy.

"Because every Tuesday I can be sure I'll be having a good meal," replied the teenager.

"We were shocked to hear this," remembers Jean-François. "Our program was not meant to provide meals for hungry children but to share knowledge and skills. But we were in one of the poorest neighbourhoods in Montreal."

This made Jean-François even more aware of the gap between rich and poor—that in a country like Canada, there are still many children going hungry.

IRON CHEF

The cooking program blossomed as kids developed an interest in good nutrition. The chefs' ideas for presenting lessons about food flew fast and furious. Why not link high-school kids with first-graders to start them learning about good nutrition even earlier?

The big end-of-year contest was fashioned after the television program *Iron Chef*. Many student contestants were challenged to create a meal using only the ingredients presented to them in a prepared basket. There was no recipe included. The grand winner won the title "Iron Chef."

"I had a man on the jury who was an executive chef of a prestigious hotel," relates Jean-François. "He told me he offered a job to one of the teenagers in the competition—Maxim."

At the time, this teenager had a part-time job at a fast-food outlet.

"I saw the quality of work Maxim was doing," related the chef. "I offered him a job to do the dishes in my restaurant." He explained that the boy could pick up some good training by watching and learning the routines of a renowned kitchen. "I saw Maxim in town months after and asked how he was progressing," the chef continued. "He told me with pride that he was now cooking and hoped to become a chef himself."

Jean-François felt happy to have inspired one of the many eager teens who had registered for his classes.

FOOD FOR THOUGHT

"It's all about kids having fun around food. We're inspiring them to follow up on their interests, find their way, and learn to feed their family, which is key," says Jean-François. "This is why we do this—to help these teenagers, soon to become adults, wives, husbands, with kids of their own, to take care of themselves and follow the rules of good nutrition."

Jean-François offers his own recipe to young people who would like to make changes but don't know how to start.

"Follow your passion," he urges. "Get involved in extracurricular activities. Whether it is sports or music—or it might be cooking—you'll find an organization that needs volunteers. So volunteer! That's first. Listen to your parents—if they would like you to try community work that is out of your comfort zone, a soup kitchen for example, just go and do it. You might not like it at first, but it opens your eyes and gets your brain working."

THE ASHOKA EFFECT

"Ashoka helped me to think outside the box," says Jean-François. "At first, I was presenting my program only in Quebec, but an Ashoka Fellow asked me, 'Don't you want to involve chefs everywhere? If someone calls you from anywhere around the world and wants to share your methods, are you going to say no?'"

"It made me realize that to make a social impact, I must urge chefs toward social involvement no matter where they are located. That new way of thinking outside the box got my program to Calgary and Toronto and across North America, then into Mexico and Chile. Social impact has to be done anywhere. I think that's how we will reach a better world. Social work is completely about sharing and not taking ownership for yourself."

DAPHNE NEDERHORST
Tanzania, Africa

The Ripple Effect

Daphne Nederhorst first met Eddy when she visited Uganda. She was interested to hear about how he solved a big problem and at the same time had become a changemaker in his community. She was determined to offer him a special kind of help so he could continue to do his good work.

Eddy told Daphne about his rural village in Uganda. At the school he used to attend, children who were late or misbehaved received the "agriculture" punishment—they were sent to the field behind the school to dig up yams and clear away weeds and bushes.

"There is a piece of land at the back of the school where they send you," said Eddy, who was often late. "It felt so bad every time you came late to school. They won't listen

He had trudged out to work in that field too many times to count. It was a punishment that he'd hated.

One day, as he was out there digging in the hot sun, he had an idea. He realized he could turn his negative thoughts about farming into something positive. Knowing how to grow fruits and vegetables was actually a good skill to have.

"I had to think about how this can change things. It sparked me to start thinking about the future."

He decided to learn all he could about growing food. He started a garden of his own and soon discovered that not only did gardening provide good nutrients, it also gave him opportunities to sell his produce

Uganda, the Pearl of Africa, lies between savannah and jungle and is home to the magnificent mountain gorilla. It is a safari destination, and tourists can see prowling lions on the plains, chimpanzees in the rainforest, as well as over one thousand species of colourful birds.

The money he earned from selling his fruits and vegetables helped his family pay for their basic needs, as well as for health care and school fees.

He began to teach the local children how to cultivate fruits and vegetables so that they too could start to earn money. Soon, he wanted to share with even more people. But he was just one person. How could he share his knowledge with children in other communities?

That's when Daphne Nederhorst and her team at Sawa World stepped in.

SHARE, SHARE, AND SHARE AGAIN

Sawa World is a team of people who believe that there is a way to end poverty on our planet. The team believes that change must come from within; people have the means

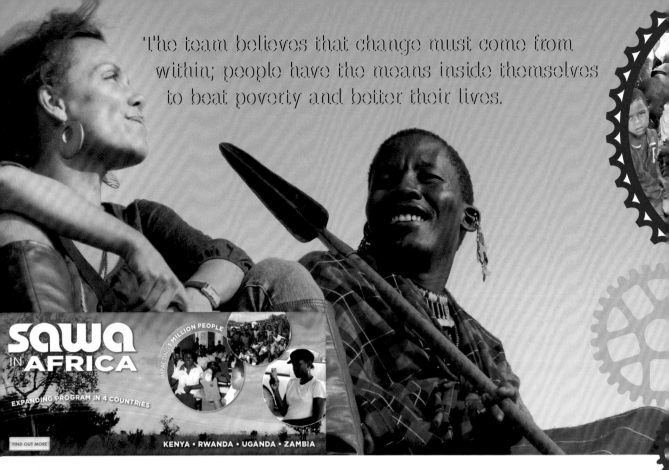

The team believes that change must come from within; people have the means inside themselves to beat poverty and better their lives.

SQWQ IN AFRICA

IMPACTING 1 MILLION PEOPLE

EXPANDING PROGRAM IN 4 COUNTRIES

FIND OUT MORE

KENYA • RWANDA • UGANDA • ZAMBIA

inside themselves to beat poverty and better their lives. One billion people around the world live in extreme poverty today[1]. Sawa World fights poverty not by giving money, but by enabling and empowering people just like Eddy—people who have found solutions and need help to share them. Founder Daphne Nederhorst leads her team to identify "sparks" like Eddy, and helps each one to create a video that shares solutions with others. Using media ensures that solutions are shared quickly and effectively among those who are seeking solutions for poverty.

Eddy is now twenty-five years old, and with Sawa World's help, he has shared his skills with schools and communities. His work is helping people to help themselves.

"So far we have fifteen people in different communities who are using the ideas about how to garden, and they are creating a passion for agriculture," says Eddy about his success. "We are creating long-lasting solutions to extreme poverty. My ultimate dream is to see the livelihoods of people change."

Sawa World leaders and volunteers spark others to help themselves—not only to grow produce, but to make candles, fashion paper beads, craft soap, keep bees...the projects are too numerous to list, but all have one thing in common—all help to defeat extreme poverty. Volunteers share the skills they have learned with others in different communities.

For Daphne, founding Sawa World was the fulfillment of a dream she'd had since childhood. "The universe gave me this mission. It's always been very clear, even as an infant," she says. "I was always very sensitive to any suffering."

A LIFELONG GOAL

Daphne was born in Holland, but her parents' work brought the family to Tanzania, and that is where she grew up. Her childhood in Africa exposed Daphne to a culture that she came to love and respect and also made her very aware of the dire poverty she saw around her. As a young child, she decided to make it her lifelong goal to help relieve suffering and poverty in the world.

It took Daphne some years to discover a way to fulfill her mission, but when she founded Sawa World, she knew right away that this would be her life's work.

Sawa World has created partnerships with people in Rwanda, Kenya, Uganda, and Zambia, and continues to reach out to millions of people by way of media technology. Daphne and her team meet with Sawa World leaders, document their work, train youth reporters, inspire new volunteers, and use the media to spread the word. Each connection energizes her team to set more goals. They want to see a world where there is no poverty and where everyone has access to clean water, shelter, and food. They want to combat problems like AIDS and other health issues. They promote gender equality among men and women. Their work helps to protect children and provide them with a basic education. Just as importantly, they want to restore and protect a damaged environment.

SIMPLE BUT TRUE

Daphne has a simple formula for children and adults who want to make changes for a better world.

"If you can envision what you want, then all it really takes is having the belief in yourself that you can do it—it is that simple!" says Daphne. "The journey begins with that. You might be falling down and standing up again a lot, but just do it with heart and integrity. The doors will open."

Daphne will continue with her work. It is, after all, a lifetime mission.

"I want to see a Sawa World where everyone has access to clean water and food," she says. "It is a ripple effect. I want this initiative to spread to people all over the world."

Sawa World continues to reach out to people, sparking inspiration and change and offering practical solutions toward ending poverty. It has already changed millions of lives.

THE ASHOKA EFFECT

"Ashoka deserves such credit! Am I really a part of this amazing organization?" enthuses Daphne. Belonging to Ashoka makes her feel as though she has become part of a large family that connects her to a global network of Fellows. "They've opened the door to funding, advisors, speaking opportunities," she says. "You realize there are other people just like you—that you're not alone."

With Ashoka's help, Sawa World has reached 4.8 million people in Uganda and continues its work in many of the poorest nations of the world. Its youth reporters have made ninety-four videos, which offer solutions to extreme poverty.

CHRIS BALME
Philadelphia, Pennsylvania, United States

Inside the Skyscrapers

It was the end of the day and nineteen-year-old Chris Balme trudged down the school's hallway toward the exit. He felt frustrated and exhausted. It had been a really tough day. As a practice teacher at a middle school, he was finding it a challenge to keep the kids interested. There were so many lost teaching moments because students just did not seem to care.

"Why do we have to learn this?" they asked. "How will this help me?"

In their opinion, school was a waste of time. Chris knew the telling statistic: one third of high-school students across the country will drop out[1]. How could he explain the importance of education to these middle- school students in a way they might really understand before it was too late? How could he tell them how vital it was that they stay in school? That the things they were learning would make a difference to their future success?

GROWING UP POOR

Chris Balme had grown up in a musical family. His parents were professional musicians, but they often struggled to make a living. In spite of this, their love of teaching was always evident. "My home was a constant flow of students," he remembers. "Both my parents were dedicated to teaching music, but it was a tough life. I saw them struggle. There were very few financial rewards that came with that life."

As a boy, Chris believed he wanted a different kind of life when he grew up, free of financial worry. "I wanted to be in control of my own destiny," he says.

Little did he know that when destiny came calling, it would take him down a far different career path than he had ever imagined.

A SKYSCRAPER OF AN IDEA

Chris chose teaching as a career. The year before his first teaching job, he studied in Paris, France. At the end of the semester, he had a great deal of time on his hands to wander about the beautiful city and explore. There was time to think.

"I had time to wonder about things—to reflect on what motivated me," remembers Chris. "I realized that I love to problem-solve. I concluded that money does not motivate me after all. It is solving problems that energizes and motivates me. That's what drew me to teaching in the first place."

Chris began his practice teaching year in that tough Philadelphia school. There he was, exhausted and discouraged after one of many difficult days. As he walked down the street, he saw the skyline of Philadelphia spread out before him, golden in the setting sun. It was a thrilling view. The tallest skyscraper was fifty-seven storeys high. All those buildings were filled with successful men and women; achievers who were enjoying the benefits of a good education.

There is such a gulf between this world and that one, he thought. *There are some great teaching resources out there, but my students' world and that one never ever connect. If only somehow they could.*

It was then that Chris had an idea. Each one of those office towers was filled with the potential for learning. There were producers, artists, architects—a whole selection of careers were represented by the many people who worked inside. What if kids could actually go into those workplaces to learn? Such an experience would kick-start their waning interests, show them the practical uses of a good education, and put them back on track.

"I kept thinking about those middle-school kids who didn't understand why education is important."

Chris knew he wanted to build an organization that would change the attitudes of those kids. Because Chris wanted to fan the inner sparks of possibility in each student, he called his new endeavour "Spark."

The bustling city of Philadelphia has a magnificent skyline. There are 381 highrises, and the tallest of these is 57 meters high. In this city in 1776, the members of the Thirteen American Colonies met and declared their separateness from Britain by signing the Declaration of Independence. As a result, the United States of America was born.

SPARKING A CHANGE

Today, Chris Balme's idea has become a reality. Spark offers an apprenticeship program to students who are in danger of dropping out. Many of these students have the skills but are not applying them—they don't see why they should. Now they have the golden opportunity to meet with experts and learn first-hand from them—mentors who are successful in their chosen careers. For teenagers in the program, Spark is the chance of a lifetime, but the selection process is finely tuned.

"In all referrals, we train teachers and counselors to look for a profile—students who are clearly struggling. We don't want the best academic students," says Chris.

When the team has selected the students, they ask each candidate this question: If you could try any career in the world, what career would you choose?

Once the students have named their interest, the team matches each teenager with a mentor who is already successful in that field. For a few hours each week, students work with their apprentice teacher right in the workplace.

"Students who are ready to take the responsibility of going into a workplace can explore what certain jobs entail," Chris explains. "There is so much potential among these kids to engage."

When the work experience is completed, students present all they have learned to their parents, teachers, and friends.

The results are amazing. "A lot of kids are struggling in school and may not appear to be respectful, but if you give them a chance, there is a total personal transformation. In the workplace, you suddenly see a curious, respectful person," says Chris. "We grew to be less surprised at these transformations, but teachers and parents were the most surprised." The kids who had the least interest in learning were now totally engaged in learning.

The young learners finally understand that to reach a career goal, education really matters. Parents and teachers learn that these young people are not hopeless after all. They realize that there is the spark of potential in every young person, no matter the difficulties.

LISA'S STORY

Chris remembers Lisa, who was homeless and living in a car. Her circumstances made it hard for her to concentrate in class. She was failing and struggling to stay afloat. In her Spark interview, she told the team she would like to be a movie director.

"We matched her with a person who directed trailers at 20th Century Fox," says

Chris. "I was there for her first day. I'll never forget it. They showed her a movie trailer for a film not yet released and asked her to critique it. She watched it and launched into a sophisticated critique. Right away, the director called in his team and they took out their note pads and jotted down every word she said. They were genuinely interested."

Lisa eventually produced a movie trailer for 20th Century Fox to demonstrate the skills she had learned. Needless to say, her confidence soared, and she achieved A's in her academic work from then on.

There are hundreds of success stories. Lisa's is only one of the many journeys that middle-school kids have experienced through Spark.

What is your dream job? Do you want to learn more about it? Chris has advice for you. "The resources to learn are everywhere.

You can find them. The opportunities are all around us. There are all kinds of cool things. Just ask for permission to come and learn. It's a lot easier than it sounds."

THE ASHOKA EFFECT

"Being a social entrepreneur can be lonesome," says Chris. "You sometimes feel like it's all impossible! So it really helps to have the affirmation of other people—this amazing network of people at Ashoka."

The team at Spark enjoys the opportunity to share their knowledge with those in other countries. They have talked to educators in Kenya and Brazil, and they continue to seed their idea into more locations around the United States.

CHANTELLE & SONAM
BUFFIE SWARUP
Vancouver, British Columbia, Canada

The Kabobs, the Cooks, and the Recipe for Success

Two cooks bent over a hot stove working as fast as they could. Chantelle and Sonam were preparing food for one hundred people at an event in downtown Vancouver, and they were already one hour late. The pakoras and lentils were only half finished, and they had not even started the kabobs. Even if they finished soon, it would take time to transport the food to the event.

Then the phone rang. It was the event organizers.

"Where are you? You're late! We're all waiting."

In between fielding more urgent phone calls from the company who had hired them as caterers, they raced frantically about the small kitchen, mentally preparing themselves

Chantelle paused for a moment, wondering what to do. *We've taken on too much work, and we've let everyone down*, she thought.

It was a low moment for two people who up until then, hadn't known failure.

THE SHACK ACROSS THE STREET

Chantelle Buffie was born in Canada o Filipino, Austrian, and French-Canadia descent. When she was eight, she visited family in the Philippines and experienced a culture very different from the Canadia culture that she knew. She was fascinated with the festivals and customs and especially the food with its Spanish and Asian influences She also noticed the stark differences in the her relatives in a comfortable home, across the street she saw a shack on the riverbank and a mother struggling to give her two children the basic needs of food, clothing, and shelter.

How can there be such differences among people who only live across the street from each other? she wondered.

Her experience in the Philippines and her curiosity about the world and its inequities stayed with her, even when she became a student in the business program at Simon Fraser University in Vancouver.

DYNAMITE DUO

While at university, Chantelle befriended Sonam Swarup. Sonam had spent a summer teaching inner-city students in Ecuador, and exotic travel was one of many interests these two young women shared. They also shared a passion for authentic ethnic food. Each believed that food was the way to bridge gaps between cultures; food was a language that everyone understood.

Vancouver is a city of culturally diverse groups of people—Punjabi, Chinese, German, Italian, to name only a few. To help the city celebrate such diversity, Chantelle and Sonam were asked to cater a Vancouver multicultural festival. With some help, the two were sure they could manage it.

The contract looked easy enough: serve appetizers to one hundred people. They decided on Pakistani cuisine. They calculated the ingredients, planned their menu, and on the day of the event, they set to work.

It was then that things began to go terribly wrong. Chantelle and Sonam had miscalculated the time it would take to prepare so many appetizers. Now they were already one hour late and were only halfway

Diwali is a Sanskrit word meaning "row of lights." The festival of lights is celebrated by Hindus, Jains, and Sikhs around the world every autumn after the summer harvest. It is especially observed in Nepal and India and symbolizes the victory of light over darkness. A happy holiday, it includes thousands of lights shining in communities wherever it is celebrated.

through the food preparation. Worse, it would take them another forty minutes to transport the appetizers. Chantelle and Sonam stopped in the middle of the preparation and, in a panic, called their mentor at the university to ask for advice. He told them that even though they had failed, the best and only thing to do now was to control their reaction to failure and to keep a positive mindset. After all, the two had not totally failed. The food would be delivered even though it was late. They could still try to make a great impression. Failure is not final.

Heartened by the advice, the two completed the appetizers, and with confident smiles and sincere apologies for the delay, they delivered the trays of food.

MIX IT, TASTE IT, TALK ABOUT IT

As part of their university-course require-ments, Chantelle and Sonam developed ideas about bringing employment skills to immigrant women. Together, they designed Fusion Kitchen—a program that would build connections among cultures and highlight cultural differences in a positive way.

"I don't really call myself a cook," explains Chantelle, "but Sonam and I are always hungry for ethnic food, for new experiences, and for travel to different cultures."

In the Fusion Kitchen, immigrant women offered cooking lessons to interested students and demonstrated how to prepare the food that they enjoyed in their homeland. Special recipes with the rich flavours these immigrant women had known since they were children are shared. Not only did it build their self-confidence, but it also gave these new Canadians work experience they could put on their résumés—something that is valuable for finding a full-time job.

The project was going well. Ashoka provided financial help and mentorship, and already a few women who had only recently arrived in Canada were giving cooking classes. These new Canadians were sharing the cuisine of their home culture to interested students, teaching them how to mix the special ingredients and spices to create meals with an ethnic flavour. At the same time, the women were polishing their English-language skills and building valuable work experience.

FESTIVAL OF LIGHTS

After a successful year at university, Chantelle and Sonam were able to use that experience of failing during their "catering crisis" to create success. They accepted a contract to offer three cooking classes that would help chefs prepare for the Vancouver Diwali Festival—a celebration of life, goodness, and enjoyment. At this "Festival of Lights,"

Chantelle and Sonan shone as brightly as the lamps and candles that lit up the festival.

They were on time, and they delivered.

The two reflected on their eventual success. "These moments of doubt, fear, and failure have shaped us. We can embrace our weaknesses because we've learned from them. Failure is never final. It is a learning opportunity."

Chantelle and Sonam live this advice every day. In recognition for their work, they were honoured with a "Top 24 Under 24" award, which is given to selected young social entrepreneurs in Vancouver. Chantelle continues to gain national recognition for her visionary leadership. In 2014, she was selected for "The Next 36"—a program that recognizes the contributions of young entrepreneurs and helps them build on their vision for innovative change. Chosen from thousands of applicants across Canada each year, thirty-six young entrepreneurs build companies with the help of business advisors and mentors.

Although Fusion Kitchen is no longer operating—Chantelle and Sonam have moved on to other initiatives—the big picture has not changed. "I see myself as always giving back to the community in some way. I always want to help people," says Chantelle. Sonam echoes this sentiment as she continues her university studies.

Chantelle advises young people who have an idea for change to ask for help. "You don't need to know all the answers," she says. "There are people who can help. Don't think that because you're young, you can't do it. There are lots of children and young people who are doing amazing things."

Will you be one of them? If you have an idea for change, ask for help. You will be surprised at all the doors that will open for you.

THE ASHOKA EFFECT

"Ashoka provided financial support and mentoring for Fusion Kitchen," says Chantelle. "The organization helped sponsor a competition at the beginning and helped with our funding. They connected us to other social entrepreneurs who shared their insights with us. Having this support helped us build awareness of multicultural influences. It helped us to explore and educate people about the cultural diversity in our community."

STANLEY ZLOTKIN
Toronto, Ontario, Canada

Some Sprinkles On That?

he two-seater plane skimmed the treetops, landed, and taxied along a grass landing strip. Inside the cabin, a young doctor gazed out of the dusty window, catching a glimpse of bare-skinned Nigerian tribesmen and women. They stood along the side of the runway, and from their vantage point, stared with a level of curiosity equal to his. Once the plane came to a halt, the cabin door swung open, letting in a blast of heat from the scorching temperature outside.

This was Dr. Stanley Zlotkin's first connection with the tribal people of a developing nation, and he felt both scared and exhilarated. As part of his practicum, the twenty-two-year-old had committed to three months in this remote area of Africa. He would soon begin

learning about the challenges of delivering medical care in a hospital with limited supplies and no electricity. He would learn how people coped when there was not enough food.

THE KID FROM TORONTO

Even as a young boy, Stanley had been fascinated with the history of medicine, and especially with germs and science.

"I read all I could. I had an innate interest in science and discovery. My uncle was a doctor and I modelled myself after him," he explains.

Stanley's experiences in Nigeria were to strengthen him as a person and a physician.

"I had no choice but to approach the challenge with gusto," recounts Stanley. "The plane wasn't coming back for three months.

I had to make the best of a difficult situation."

There were only two nurses at the mission hospital where he worked, and to them he was "the kid from Toronto" who had never travelled before. But by applying the problem-solving skills he had been taught in medical school, he learned how to set priorities and how to be self-sufficient in a difficult physical environment.

"I was young and impressionable, and I survived it and learned there is another life on Earth outside the West. It was a life-changing experience for me," says Stanley. "But at first, I was scared out of my pants!"

Armed with this experience and following a further few years of training in pediatric medicine, Dr. Zlotkin continued to apply his problem-solving skills to new challenges.

A KITCHEN EXPERIMENT

World hunger concerned him, and Stanley became very interested in solving the problem of "hidden hunger" among the children of developing nations.

All growing children have a vital need for iron, zinc, and other important minerals supplied in meat and dairy products. However, children in developing countries may not have access to nutritious food. These children may not feel hungry, but their diet does not contain all the vitamins and minerals that they need in order to grow strong and healthy.

Known as "hidden hunger," this vitamin and mineral deficiency during the first few years of a child's life can lead to major health problems later on. Without proper nutrition, children's immune systems suffer, and they become more prone to infections. Their brains do not develop as quickly as the brains of well-nourished children, their growth rate slows, and they experience learning problems that lead to less productive lives.

Finding a solution took Stanley countless

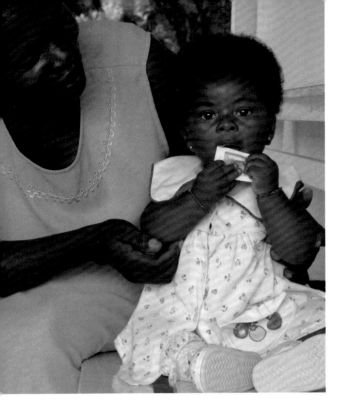

Children often need specialized treatment for illnesses, and The Hospital for Sick Children, also known as SickKids, has been meeting these needs since 1875. This hospital in Toronto, Canada, is a hospital of "firsts"!

★ In 1892, it became the first hospital to house a school so that children could continue to learn while they were receiving treatment.

★ It was the first hospital to install a solar thermal energy system on the rooftop. The system heats up the hospital's hot water supply and reduces energy costs.

★ The hospital's research institute is renowned worldwide. Every day, two thousand scientists and doctors perform groundbreaking research into childhood cancer, cystic fibrosis, and other diseases.

hours of work and experimentation. Often, he worked all night in the kitchen of The Hospital for Sick Children in Toronto.

The solution he eventually found was a surprisingly simple one.

His invention, Sprinkles, consists of tiny capsules filled with vitamins and minerals packaged in little paper packets. Caregivers in developing nations where hidden hunger is prevalent sprinkle the packet contents onto the children's semi-solid food, mixing it well. The important vitamins and minerals that a child needs are instantly delivered with ease, and no change is made to the taste of the meal.

FROM A TENT IN MONGOLIA

Today, Sprinkles has successfully reached thirty million children and the number is growing. Stanley's invention has taken him to many countries around the world. He remembers his first test case in Mongolia. There, nomadic families that live in tents,

herd cattle, and follow their grazing animals were successfully using Sprinkles, and had good things to say about it.

"Have you seen any differences in your child since adding Sprinkles to food?" Stanley asked one of the mothers.

She certainly had noticed big differences.

"Before, my child was lethargic," she replied. "But in two or three weeks, my child started acting normal."

She went on to describe her ambitions for her children. "I want them to have an education, some security, a hut of their own so they can be out of the rain, to be married, healthy, and happy."

Stanley realized that no matter their religious beliefs—whether they were Christians, Muslims, or Buddhists—parents around the world all wanted the same things for their children.

"No family says, 'We want our country to be at war,' or 'we want our children to be

sick,'" says Stanley. "Individual people want the same things for their children, no matter where they live. It taught me to always think globally about people's needs."

Stanley has advice for all young changemakers of today.

"Start small," he says. "There is no project that's too small to make a difference. You will be discouraged if it's a huge idea. Making change is a step-by-step process. But don't give up your thoughts about making a difference, even if the thought is very small. Be creative, and don't let anyone turn off your creativity," he advises. "We must always remember how fortunate we are in Canada," he adds, "and start by giving back to our own community."

THE ASHOKA EFFECT

The food supplement Sprinkles is now available in sixty-two countries, and thirty million children are being reached each year.

"Sprinkles is being championed by a number of United Nations agencies; the two biggest are UNICEF and the World Food Program," says Stanley. "Having the right partnerships and the right marketing has played a huge role."

One of those partners has been Ashoka.

"With Ashoka's support, I had a feeling of comfort that there are other people like me doing similar things," he says. "Not only the Canadians who are doing fabulous, important things for other people, but people around the world thinking as entrepreneurs—that what they're doing can be sustained and used in local situations and country situations.

I've always had a sense of well-being when I'm among people who are doing very similar things that I've done, whose values are the same as my own."

Dr. Zlotkin is thrilled to have these partnerships. "I'm astonished whenever I see a new Sprinkles program being started and feel humbled that it started locally in my brain. It's a great pleasure to be a champion for the invention, and it's just as important to have found the right partners. We are all doing something of value that is sustainable and is making a difference in the community. With Ashoka, I'm part of a bigger community that has similar ideas around social entrepreneurships."

He has since introduced a new product, SuppleFem, which is providing important supplements to the diet of pregnant women. All profits go back into the project.

LOUISE DAVIS LANGHEIER
San Francisco, California, USA

You Have a Voice

ouise Davis Langheier knew early on that she liked giving to others. While observing the world around herself, she realized that every person has special needs as well as special gifts. When she was little, she watched her parents give to others in very different ways.

"My dad reminded us to count our blessings, and that we should always give to the other person—ask them how they are doing, what do they need," she remembers. "He taught me to always be helpful to others. My mom was passionate about food and she looked out for others to make sure they had enough to eat. She helped out at the food banks and helped deliver food to community centres and homeless shelters."

These constant lessons from her parents influenced Louise to find her own way to help others.

When the AIDS virus began to strike down so many victims, Louise felt angry and sad about it. She volunteered for an organization that offered help to those suffering from HIV/AIDS. Through her work, she met teenagers her own age who had made the wrong health decisions, which led to their lives being forever changed. She realized that if only these teenagers had had the right tools to help them make good decisions, their lives would have been so different.

"I wanted to act on it immediately," she says.

FIND YOUR VOICE

Today, Louise continues to act on her empathy for those in distress. She has established Peer Health Exchange—an organization that teaches students about good health practices and much more. It encourages high-school students to find their voices and speak up.

Because of budget cuts, many public schools in the United States are no longer offering health education and, as a result, students now lack the guidance to make responsible choices and find their way[1]. They are taking big risks with their personal health and well-being. With no guidance or support, teens are making choices that could affect them in a negative way for the rest of their lives—drug experimentation and addiction, STDs, smoking, binge drinking, or unwanted pregnancies could be the result. Teenagers who engage in risky behaviour are more likely to drop out of school, putting their futures at risk.

Louise founded Peer Health Exchange as a way to give young adults their voices. It teaches them that it is okay to speak up and define one's boundaries—that teens do not have to let their peers pressure them into taking risks. She believes that education is not just there to provide knowledge, but also to give children a foundation for life. Louise offers more than health education. Her program offers life skills that will stay with the students and help determine how they will direct their lives in the future.

THE ROAD TO GOOD HEALTH

Peer Health Exchange is a group of university volunteers who work with underprivileged high-school students in schools that do not have a health-education program. Because these volunteers are closer in age to the

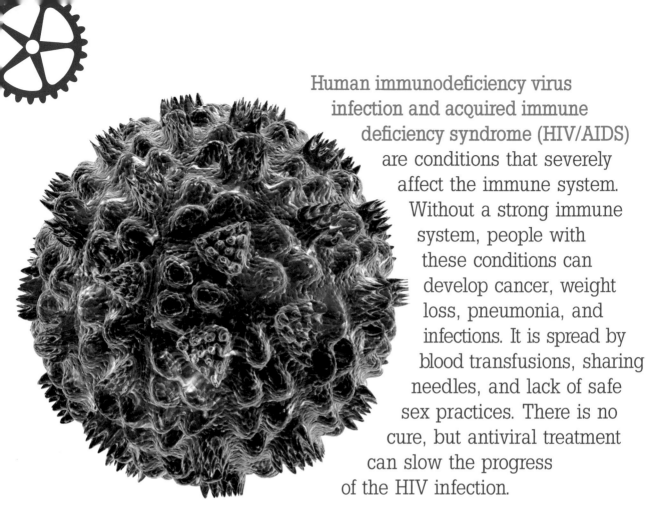

Human immunodeficiency virus infection and acquired immune deficiency syndrome (HIV/AIDS) are conditions that severely affect the immune system. Without a strong immune system, people with these conditions can develop cancer, weight loss, pneumonia, and infections. It is spread by blood transfusions, sharing needles, and lack of safe sex practices. There is no cure, but antiviral treatment can slow the progress of the HIV infection.

high-school students, it is easier for them to become mentors and role models. When at-risk students work with these successful and goal-oriented university students, they begin to understand how important it is to stay on track and to keep their own values and goals in sight. They learn about sexual health, relationships, substance abuse, good nutrition, physical fitness, and mental health.

Students learn how to deal with negative peer pressure. When school friends urge them to try drugs, they learn how to speak up, and how to resist pressures that could bring them harm. They explore their own personal goals and the things they value most in their lives.

Volunteers ask the students some soul-searching questions: What would it mean to them if they lost these goals and values that are most important to them—that define their very identity? How deeply would it change their lives?

Armed with this new knowledge about themselves, the students have a framework for the rest of their lives. They emerge stronger and more powerful, able to resist negative influences and to keep their eyes on the goal.

One student who benefitted from the program told Louise: "I've never spoken up for myself, or been able to say what I wanted

to my friends. Now I feel I have some voice to say what I want to the people I care about. I feel comfortable telling them I don't want to do it and why. It's my decision to make."

Now, Peer Health Exchange is helping over 17,000 teens across the country.

"Helping young people to realize their agency and find their voice is so important to the work we do," says Louise. "I'm thrilled when we have a teen walking out of our program who can use that voice—know it's theirs to do what is right for them."

Louise has a lot of advice for young changemakers. "Figure out what you care about the most—what interests you. You will be most successful at making a difference when you feel connected to something meaningful."

Louise has a unique approach to her life's work. "Suppose I only have today," she says. "What would I do with it? How would I want to experience the world? If you look at each day in this way, there's a lot of power in that."

THE ASHOKA EFFECT

"Ashoka has allowed me to do the work—to keep with it and not feel limited by financial constraints," says Louise. "Meeting other entrepreneurs has allowed me to learn from some of the best minds in the field. I have an incredible network of people to draw upon. I've become more effective at what I do and feel support beyond just the financial borders."

Peer Health Exchange was founded in 2004. The majority of high-school students that have participated in it say that even as the program was running, they were already beginning to make healthier decisions. High-school principals are so impressed with the program, they are recommending it to other schools. As a result, dozens of schools are on the waiting list for Peer Health Exchange.

JOAQUIN LEGUIA
Lima, Peru, South America

The Children's Forests

The clouds overhead seemed close enough to touch. Joaquin (Wa-keen') Leguia scrambled up the trunk of the mahogany tree as high as he could go and from his perch, he stretched out his hand, trying to grab some fluffy whiteness for himself. He was only four, and in his imagination, the little field outside his home with the blue sky above was a garden of delight. He imagined that his dogs were lions and tigers and he was Tarzan, running barefoot over the grass. His older brother had an imagination equal to Joaquin's and together, they captured wild animals and had amazing adventures. "I was Indiana Jones without the whip," remembers Joaquin. Often the two brothers pretended they were famous soccer players and scored the winning goal as roaring crowds clapped and cheered.

Sister moon, Mother sun, and Brother stars all helped Joaquin to be himself and find rest, amusement, and happiness in the magical garden. If he felt sad, the sun would dry his tears. When his mother called him to do his homework, the wild garden gave him a hiding place. When he was angry, he kicked a tree just once—and quickly learned he was only hurting himself. When he was given a gun for a birthday present and carelessly shot a bird, he buried the bird and the gun and vowed never to kill again. He didn't know it yet, but the garden was teaching him lessons that would stay with him forever.

RAINFOREST ADVENTURES

While he was still a boy, Joaquin's parents divorced and his remaining family began a new life in the city of Lima near the Amazon rainforest.

It wasn't long before he became friends with three Shipibo boys who knew the jungle and all its mysteries and who demonstrated love and respect for the land. They helped him learn about the animals of the forest and what their sounds meant. They cautioned him about safety.

"Walk this way," they would teach. "You almost stepped on a poisonous snake!" They showed him how to paddle against the river's current and how to catch fish. They advised him not to be fearful of nature, just to be aware and to feel nature in a different way. They firmly and caringly taught Joaquin to be safe but never to feel afraid in the rainforest.

The lessons he learned in the rainforest added to his knowledge of nature. It's no wonder Joaquin Leguia later chose a career path that brought him close to nature!

But there were some roadblocks along the way.

His father was a politician, his mother was a businesswoman, and his grandfather had twice been president of Peru. The pressure was on Joaquin to become either a politician or a Wall Street banker.

At first, Joaquin did what was expected of him and took business courses at university, but it didn't feel right for him and he was failing. At the age of twenty-five, he studied at Yale University, and a wise professor advised him to follow his heart.

"The environment has a great impact upon children. I want to study this important relationship."

The professor gave him his full support—the first time anyone ever had.

"I learned the meaning of the word 'recognition,'" he says. "Someone was telling me to listen to my heart."

Children's Forests is the result. Joaquin and his team bring children together with gardens to teach them how to take care of the land. The Amazon rainforest is in trouble because of the farmers and loggers that cut down trees and clear the land. Natural habitats are being destroyed. Joaquin helps children to understand and appreciate nature and gives them skills to become

conservationists. Whether in a rural or urban landscape, on a roof or in a backyard, on a beach or in the mountains, just a few square metres of land can make a world of difference in every child's life.

THE RULE OF THREE

"In Children's Forests, each child starts by learning to plant three different things: one for themselves, one for others, and one for the environment," explains Joaquin. "For example, a child might plant oregano for herself because she likes pizza, a healing plant to give to a sick grandfather, and a red flower that hummingbirds like."

They team up with their parents, with their teachers, and with conservation professionals to learn about the environment.

Joaquin is using his political knowledge to make changes. He wants the government of Peru to recognize that children have the right to enjoy the natural environment. He asks that parts of the forest be set aside for children's use. If all children learn to become stewards of the land, they will keep those skills for the rest of their lives. As adults, they will pass on their knowledge and respect for the environment to their own children.

"When kids see what grows and stays planted, it strengthens their self-confidence and the skills they possess to create positive change in society. It gives them access to a better quality of life," says Joaquin.

ANIA: SPIRIT OF THE GARDEN

Joaquin remembers how his childhood garden was eventually paved over to make a tennis court. "I was sad, but somehow the spirit of the garden went to live within me," he says. "Every child should have a little place where they can be in a natural environment, where they

can find bees, feel nature, and do what they believe in by nurturing the land around them. That is the purpose of Children's Forests."

Joaquin has a rich, full laugh, and when he speaks there is laughter in his voice, but he becomes very serious as he thinks about his advice for you. "We have all come with a purpose in this life, no matter what profession we choose. You can be a dancer, a soccer player, an artist, a banker, but for everyone, our purpose is all the same—to make a better world!" he says.

THE ASHOKA EFFECT

"William Burch, a great ecologist and my advisor from Yale University, was a big influence in my life. After him, it was Ashoka," Joaquin says.

Joaquin had always found it difficult to define himself, but Ashoka changed that.

"Even when I graduated from Yale, I still didn't know the answer to this question: What am I? I have always been a wild card, but Ashoka saw the real me and understood me. It was the people at Ashoka who told me, 'You're a social entrepreneur,'" he explains.

"As soon as I heard that, I knew that's exactly what I am! Ashoka gave me that recognition and acknowledgment."

So far, twenty million children have transformed two million acres of land and Joaquin and his team continue with new initiatives.

AMY BARZACH
South Windsor, Connecticut, USA

Over, Under, Around & Through

It was a warm, sunny day at the park. A little girl sat and watched the children playing on the playground. There were swings, slides, monkey bars, rings, and ladders. The children were having lots of fun, laughing and shouting to one another. She wanted so much to join in, but she couldn't.

The playground didn't have any places for a little girl in a wheelchair to play.

Amy Barzach watched the little girl and understood how left out she must have felt. The scene tugged at her heartstrings. Amy had always felt concern for others, especially those in need.

When she was a little girl, Amy had set up a lemonade stand in her driveway, just like many other boys and girls who wanted to make some money on a summer day had.

But Amy's stand was special. The money she earned went to a children's charity. If there were not enough customers to fill up her money can, she would put in her own money so that she would have enough to give.

LEFT OUT

In high school, Amy developed a condition known as scoliosis, and for a while, she needed to wear a back brace with long metal poles that went from her hips to her neck. She experienced first-hand the feeling of being different from others—excluded from games and fun.

In university, she continued her practice of helping others by reading course material to a blind student and always looking out for the needs of those less able. Her first son

Scoliosis is a curvature of the spine, a condition that can happen in children during a growth spurt just before puberty. Some children may need a brace to stop the curvature from getting worse, while others may need surgery.

Jonathan, suffered from a weakening of the muscles known as spinal muscular atrophy. Sadly, he died within the year.

Amy remembered the little girl in the wheelchair who could not play with the others on the playground. She remembered how she had felt when she was suffering from scoliosis and could not take part in many school activities. She wanted to honour her son's memory and could think of no better way to do so than to build a playground where all children could play, no matter their abilities.

A PLAYGROUND FOR EVERYONE

Amy and her husband asked for donations and the help of thousands of volunteers to build a playground that she named "Jonathan's Dream." She knew that Jonathan would have wanted all children to be able to join in and play with others. The playground had enough room for a child in a wheelchair to use it easily. The community loved it, and it became the model for new designs.

Amy called the model "The Boundless Playground" because children of all abilities could use it.

Jonathan's Dream was the first inclusive playground in the United States, and the idea has spread to Canada and other parts of the world.

What does a Boundless Playground look like? Imagine a place where every child can reach the highest level because every level is accessible, where swings and bouncers have back support, and where sand tables are built higher so children in wheelchairs can use them. Imagine textures and sounds that can be touched and heard for sight- or hearing-impaired children, and mazes and gardens for all to enjoy. This is the playground that Amy and her team have created—one that breaks down both physical and social barriers, a place where all children can play together.

A BOAT SWING WITH A DIFFERENCE

Amy remembers one of the children who enjoyed the inclusive playground. Matthew suffered from a disease that resulted in the curvature of his joints and left him in a wheelchair. From the age of six, he would watch from the edge of the playground, wishing that he could join in. He longed for a glider-boat swing that he could enter easily from his wheelchair, but there was no such swing in the playground. When he was older, he asked Amy if she could build a more inclusive playground at his old elementary school. He had asked the right person! With her helpers, Amy was able to provide an inclusive playground, complete with a glider-boat swing. Matthew was in high school now, but he revisited the playground. It was called "Friendship Place" because Matthew wanted everyone who played on it to enjoy friendship, no matter their abilities.

"The smile on his face was something I'll never forget," says Amy, describing Matthew's first look at the new inclusive playground. Matthew went on to university, confident of his abilities in spite of his physical challenges.

This is only one of the many success stories surrounding Boundless Playgrounds.

Amy talks about the qualities needed to be a changemaker. She offers four pieces of advice.

"Open your eyes! There are needs all around you," she urges. "If you identify something that needs to be done in the world you're living in right now, you're best positioned to do something about it.

"Listen to and talk to the people who are affected by this issue. Find out what their hopes and dreams are. In a perfect world, what would it look like?

"Turn the challenge around—whatever the challenge. When Matthew was in middle school, he saw children who were not able to play just sitting on the sidelines. See the problem as he did. Talk to people. Imagine that if you could solve this problem what it might look like."

Amy's final piece of advice mirrors the way children move on a playground. "Over, under, around, and through," she says. "There are obstacles you run into, dead ends, but go over, under, around, or through. You can get to a place where you can make things happen."

THE ASHOKA EFFECT

"Ashoka was an incredible part of my whole experience," says Amy. "When I first connected with Ashoka, it was 2002. I didn't realize there was a whole community of other changemakers—other people looking to make things better and improve the world in big and small ways. As part of a community of other changemakers, I got support for when I hit roadblocks. Things are not perfectly easy. You're trying to change a system, so having other allies, the world, the environment—all that helped to be a catalyst for me. Instead of one playground, we created a new national standard that has impacted people all over the world, not just in the US."

Amy continues to expand her vision for Boundless Playgrounds, tackling the problems of childhood obesity, breaking down barriers between people with and without disabilities, and enabling opportunities for social tolerance.

KAMAL MOUZAWAK
Beirut, The Lebanese Republic

Make Food, Not War

If you live in a peaceful country, you probably take peace for granted in your daily life. But there are many war-torn countries in the world where life is not so certain. In Lebanon, where a civil war raged for years, many lost their lives. Children growing up there experienced the fear and uncertainty of daily conflict. Born in Lebanon, Kamal Mouzawak was one of these children. Civil war was a fact of life for him. As a result, he became keenly aware of life's fragility.

THE PROBLEM WITH WAR

Kamal was born on a farm in Lebanon. The country has fertile soil for farming, but during Kamal's childhood, instead of growing crops, the soil was strewn with land mines. All around him, a civil war was tearing apart his country. The noise of guns and rocket fire filled the air.

Lebanon has always been a land of religious, ethnic, and cultural differences. Before the civil strife, Christians, Muslims, Druze, Kurds, Armenians, and refugees from Palestine lived peacefully side by side within its borders. But during the civil war, farmers were unable to farm and tensions sprang up among its peoples.

Aware of the family's need to experience a measure of peace, Kamal's grandmother made sure the large family came to the kitchen table to share their meals. The food she prepared was so delicious that each member felt valued and calm in the oasis of

peace she created around the table.

Because of the civil war, however, farming became difficult, and many farmers found it easier to simply leave their farms and start new lives in the city. As a result, fresh fruit and vegetables became hard to find and too expensive for many to buy. Lebanon was becoming a land of fast food, leading to both obesity and malnutrition. Even worse, the Lebanese people were losing their knowledge of how to prepare traditional food.

At the end of the war, when Kamal was older, he remembered how his family had gathered around the table and found a peaceful haven there as they shared their family meal. He used his childhood experiences to find a solution and bring farmers together again in peace, in spite of their religious and cultural differences.

MARKET OF GOOD

Just as Kamal's large family had gathered around the kitchen table, Lebanese farmers of different religions and cultures are now gathering together at a special marketplace to sell their produce. Kamal calls this gathering Souk el-Tayeb, or "The Market of Good." He believes that one way toward achieving lasting peace in Lebanon is through a love and appreciation of its native food. Time is proving him right.

Linked to the market is a restaurant that offers the traditional foods of Lebanon using ingredients cultivated by local farmers. Here, visitors taste delicious food and at the same time learn about traditional Lebanese dishes. In this way, farmers are preserving not only their livelihoods, but also their important traditions.

But Kamal and his team did not stop there. The ideas were flowing. One of these, the Souk and Schools program, has enriched the

One way toward achieving lasting peace in Lebanon is through a love and appreciation of its native food.

curriculum by linking students with the land and the country's food traditions. School children learn to prepare a meal "from garden to table," or they visit communities to learn about traditional cooking and culture.

The results of Kamal's many projects are amazing. Farmers are returning to cultivate the land, and tourists are visiting communities to enjoy delicious traditional meals, crafts, and music.

If you were to ask Kamal how he manages to bring together people who were in conflict with one another, he would reply that everyone is united by a common ground: the transforming power of cuisine.

"We never highlight conflict resolution. We find the common ground and look for similarities among our differences," he explains.

That common ground, of course, is the enjoyment of traditional cooking.

"Make food, not war" is Kamal's mantra for success.

Kamal's advice to young people is simple: "Bring the best contribution you can to life. Each one of us should be a changemaker—we're adding nothing to life if we aren't," he says. "It's not about winning a prize or being known. It's just about any change that we can do at any level, small or big. Make a change for the better."

Kamal refers to the real meaning of kung fu—the art of doing something well, a skill achieved through hard work. "Whatever you do, do it well," he advises.

THE ASHOKA EFFECT

"Ashoka is a platform that permitted us to get in touch with others," says Kamal. "It's a wonderful platform that puts you in contact with people around the world. You become part of a network, and you receive recognition that confirms that you should do more and even better."

Kamal and his team continue to use cuisine to help transform communities, not only in Lebanon, but in other parts of the world, too.

MICHELLE LEM
Ottawa, Ontario, Canada

The Doc, the Pets, and the Meaning of Happiness

It's not only pets that are cared for by Michelle Lem, Doctor of Veterinary Medicine and founder of Community Veterinary Outreach. She helps people, too: the young woman who left an abusive situation at home and took her two dogs with her; the bipolar youth who relied on his dog to tell him through its body language when he was swinging into a manic state; the drug addict who sold his dog to buy more drugs but then felt so sick about it, he stole his dog back and gave up drugs; the young boy rescued from living on the street, his family broken, his dog unwelcome, and his brother overdosing on drugs. There are so many troubled humans and their animals that Michelle has reached out to, and there are hundreds more. She and her team of care workers have effected change in many lives.

But she didn't always have a clear direction for her life's work.

NEVER GOOD ENOUGH

Michelle Lem's high-school teachers were quick to tell her what she could not do.

"You need A's to be a vet. You're never going to be that. Better think about an alternative career choice. Your grades are not good enough."

But since the age of five, she had dreamed of a job taking care of animals. In her family, it was second nature to care for others. Volunteering came as naturally to her as breathing.

Microbiology (from the Greek, *micro*—small, and *bio*—life) is the study of extremely small forms of life, such as viruses and bacteria.

During her childhood, Michelle helped her dad host Christmas dinners for adults with cerebral palsy. She noticed the bond these people shared with their caregivers and with one another. At seventeen, Michelle volunteered at a remedial school program for children with physical and developmental challenges. *We're no different from each other,* she thought as she listened to their stories. *We're all connected. It's just luck that I don't have a disability myself.*

When she was in her early twenties, Michelle had achieved a degree in microbiology, but not without struggling. Her grades were only average, and she believed her teachers were right about her. She gave up on her dream. She was floundering, wondering what to do with her life.

An opportunity to work at a lab for animal diseases in West Africa came her way, and she travelled to Nairobi to begin. But once there, she was unhappy to find herself gazing through the small lens of a microscope instead of looking at the big picture and following her natural desire to help others.

GRAB THAT DREAM

A moment of reflection in that Nairobi lab changed Michelle's life. *This is wrong for me,* she realized. *My work is too narrow. What about the people who own these animals?*

She observed that Kenyan farmers live closely with their cattle. The better the health and welfare of their animals, the better the quality of life the farmers enjoyed. Their children were stronger; their income was higher. Most importantly, everyone was happier, and happiness contributes to good health.

"I want to practise veterinary medicine," she thought. "Since I gave up on that dream, I've been lost. Now I know what I want to do: use that bond between animals and people to help give both of them a better quality of life. I knew it from five years old, and I should never have thrown that away."

It wasn't too late to pick up that dream again. Several years later Michelle achieved her Doctor of Veterinary Medicine degree, and she achieved it with distinction. Her marks had soared because she had found her passion.

She travelled to New Zealand and worked in a rural clinic, giving veterinary care to people's pets, observing the bond between pets and humans and always looking at the big picture.

THE PET CONNECTION

On her return to Canada, Michelle built on her knowledge of this bond. She learned that homeless people with pets could not enter public health clinics or shelters. Since their pets were not allowed, that door to assistance was often closed to them.

Michelle later went back to school to learn more about homeless young people and their pets. She talked to two hundred street kids, ninety of whom owned pets. She wanted to find ways to bring services to those being denied help simply because they owned a cat or dog.

She learned that the homeless derive great comfort from caring for their animals and receiving unconditional love in return. Pets, the most important friends in their lives, made them feel connected and comforted. She learned many kids would rather sleep on the street with their pets than use homeless shelters where animals are forbidden. She also learned that some kids would try to get off the street to protect the well-being of their pets.

She saw kids fiercely determined to give the best care to their animal: "My pet accepts me," they told her. "I want her to be safe. If I'm not around, who will take care of my pet?"

Why not open vet clinics in church basements and community halls? There, she would offer vet service with a difference and these services would be free. She put her idea into practice. As street people waited to see her, volunteer nurse practitioners and social workers waited with them, making assessments, ready to offer the services these kids so badly needed.

When Michelle opened her first clinic, the homeless found her, and word about her spread among street people, both young and old. There were also referrals from health-care departments and social workers. Many of these new clients smoked. For the sake of the their well-being, she and her team asked them non-judgmental questions that helped them become aware of the danger of smoking around their pets.

"Is your dog exposed to secondhand smoke?" she asked. "Did you know dogs can get nasal cancers from smoke and that cats can suffer from mouth cancer?"

Michelle hoped that with these concerns, her clients would stop smoking. Pet owners knew *they* must be healthy if they wanted their pet to be healthy. Caring for their pets led to caring for themselves.

"These were proud pet owners. They would spend their last dollar on food for their pet rather than feed themselves," says Michelle. "For these people, with issues around self-esteem and acceptance, pets are a wonderful way to find unconditional love and support. A way to learn skills to manage their lives."

Michelle wishes for troubled kids to understand a simple truth: "You have to love yourself to be able to best love something else. You deserve to be happy."

Michelle is doing her part to help her clients find happiness.

THE ASHOKA EFFECT

With the help of Ashoka, Michelle provides a service that teaches life skills and engages the needy in health care and social services. Through animal care, she reaches out to First Nations people, to seniors and their pets, and to women and children exposed to domestic violence.

No one chooses to be homeless. It can happen to anyone: families, teenagers, men, and women. Over two hundred thousand Canadians today live in shelters or on the streets. Homeless Canadians usually live in poverty, have lost their jobs, or are suffering from personal conflicts or drug abuse. The Canadian government is working toward ending homelessness by providing permanent, affordable housing.

CHAPTER 17

ASHOKA

Get Started: Be the Change

The girls, boys, men, and women who are featured in this book are only a few of the many changemakers around the world. They all have something in common: they want to see a change in the world, and they work hard to make that change happen.

You too have the muscle to make a change. Can you begin to stretch that muscle? Here are some tips from changemakers to help you:

FIND YOUR PASSION

Changemakers agree that there is an important first step to create change. "Find your passion!" they urge. It is important that you have

START SMALL

Once you have an idea for change, it is not hard to develop your idea if you take it one step at a time.

LOOK AT THE BIG PICTURE

All changemakers envision the world they want to see; all believe that they can achieve that vision. They always keep their eye on the goal.

BE A LISTENER

We must listen and observe; be aware of wrongs that we can put right in some small

DIFFICULTIES CAN BE OVERCOME

Of course, there will be roadblocks along the way, but remember that you can go over, under, around, and through them.

VOLUNTEER

Volunteering to help others can give back to you in surprising ways.

ASK OTHERS FOR HELP

If you have an idea to make a change, ask for help along the way.

PRACTISE YOUR KUNG FU

Whatever change you decide to make, do it well!

WHAT CAN I DO RIGHT NOW?

What have you noticed in your school, home, or community that needs to change? Are you throwing away items in your classroom that could be reused? Can you start a compost pile in your garden? Is there a science project you would like to try that demonstrates awareness of environmental problems?

Here are some more ideas for you:

- "Turn it off" to save electricity.
- Raise funds by participating in a bake sale, then donate your earnings to help save the rainforest or to support other conservation initiatives.
- Buy recycled items.
- Bring cloth bags to the grocery store and encourage your parents to leave the car at home and walk to the supermarket.

- Instead of taking the school bus, organize a group of parents to walk to school with you and your friends every day. Try just one day each week to start. You'll be surprised by how much more you will notice about your environment, and you'll also improve your physical fitness.
- There are children around the world who are not as lucky as you. Read about the Convention on the Rights of the Child and think about ways your school can raise funds or donate learning materials.
- Finding pen pals in other countries will encourage your understanding and appreciation of other cultures. Ask your teacher for help.
- If you've noticed racism in your school, talk to your teacher about making your classroom a racism-free classroom where everyone feels valued.
- Read about people who have fought against discrimination.
- Study the contributions of people from around the world.
- Invite guest speakers from the community to talk about themselves and their work.

As the great anthropologist Margaret Mead stated, "Never doubt that a small group of thoughtful, committed citizens can change the world. Indeed, it is the only thing that ever has."

You, too, can change the world.

Believe it. Start now.

ENDNOTES

CHAPTER 3

1. "Children and Youth Risk Behaviours," last modified 30 July, 2015. Statistics Canada - Government of Canada. http://www5.statcan.gc.ca/subject-sujet/subtheme-soustheme.action?pid=20000&id=20008&lang=eng&more=0

CHAPTER 4

1. Worm, Boris, Brendal Davis, Lisa Kettemer, Christine A. Ward-Paige, Demian Chapman, Michael R. Heithaus, Steven T. Kessel, and Samuel H. Gruber. 2013. "Global catches, exploitation rates, and rebuilding options for sharks." *Marine Policy* 40 (July): 194 – 204. http://www.sciencedirect.com/science/article/pii/S0308597X13000055

2. "Managing and Reducing Waste," last modified 30 July, 2013. Environment Canada - Government of Canada. http://www.ec.gc.ca/gdd-mw/

3. The website of Shark Truth. Vancouver, B.C. http://www.sharktruth.com/

CHAPTER 5

1. "Voter Turnout at Federal Elections and Referendums," last modified 15 October 2015. Elections Canada. http://www.elections.ca/content.aspx?dir=turn&document=index&lang=e&section=ele

2. "National General Election VEP Turnout Rates, 1789-Present," last modified 11 June 2014. United States Election Project. http://www.electproject.org/national-1789-present

CHAPTER 8

1. The website of The World Hunger Education Services & Hunger Notes. Washington D.C. http://www.worldhunger.org/articles/Learn/world%20hunger%20facts%202002.htm

CHAPTER 9

1. The website of The National Centre for Education Statistics. U.S. Dept. of Education. https://nces.ed.gov/

CHAPTER 12

1. Guttamacher Institute. "State Policies in Brief: Sex and HIV Education." 1 August, 2015. Washington, D.C. http://www.guttmacher.org/statecenter/spibs/spib_SE.pdf

INDEX